No Gathering In
of this Incense

No Gathering In
of this Incense

Poems

MARK RHOADS

RESOURCE *Publications* · Eugene, Oregon

NO GATHERING IN OF THIS INCENSE
Poems

Resource Publications
An Imprint of Wipf and Stock Publishers
199 W. 8th Ave., Suite 3
Eugene, OR 97401

www.wipfandstock.com

ISBN 13: 978-1-4982-0298-5

Manufactured in the U.S.A.   01/16/2015

Acknowledgments

"Short Block," "Singing Dylan," and "Fishing" first appeared in *The Christian Science Monitor*.

"Our Old Chevy," "Plantain," and "The Occasional Fire" were first published in *The Deronda Review*.

"Telecom's Bequest," "Vital Meaning," "Legacy," and "Action Still" first appeared in *Contemporary Rhyme*.

"Main Street" first appeared in *Ballard Street Poetry Journal*.

Contents

CONTENTS

Part Two: Life in Vegas

Part Three: How to Learn

CONTENTS

Part One: Iconic Virtue

Daily I search those eyes, the windows
through which I see their future, my past, all at once.

OUR OLD CHEVY HAD NO RADIO

Our old Chevy had no radio,
no conditioned air, no seatbelts

to tie you down; so I would spread my arms
to rise out over the treeless hills,

top the pungent sage and rippling wheat,
then swoop back over the rocketing hood,

glance back into the divided glass
to see my determined mother,

my father commanding the wheel,
hell-bent for Ritzville.

My music in those generous days
was the drone of the straight six below me

the flutter of hot wind in my boyish ears,
a clattering escort of grasshoppers,

a meadowlark singing out a claim
to a fencepost.

THE SEED OF ME

My father sits on the edge of his bed in a t-shirt
angling a blue-veined foot into a leg of his pajamas.
His loins are exposed, the loins
from which the seed of me burst out
on a pleasant April night in Canyon Crest,
and afterwards he swung these feet
to the floor to sit for a moment, palms
on the mattress, his toes kneading
the cool linoleum, then looked back at my mother
to exchange a commemorative smile.
But now these pajamas claim his full attention,
one leg, then the other leg, a forced rest;
and once over his knees he labors to stand
to pull them up over his wilted buttocks;
he falls to the bed, lays his head in dry fingers,
looks down at the floor for a long, long time
as if to ponder the history of the old brown carpet.

ICONIC VIRTUE

The way my father grips those two dead squirrels
by their tails and how his left hand extends

to the barrel-end of a rifle, butt at his feet; and those
dungarees and the work shirt he is wearing, the way

he has rolled up his sleeves; and my mother,
how she stands next to my father in tailored slacks

and a waste-length sweater; and the way that squirrel
hangs from her left hand, held by her thumb

and first two fingers; even how she tucks her thumb
in under the fingers of her right hand

as it hangs at her side; and how young they look,
clowning around in front of this old cabin;

and how they both smile, draws me as the icon
of a saint draws the devout to consider the origins

of a virtue. Daily I search those eyes, the windows
through which I see their future, my past, all at once.

SNOW

sifts through a ghostly stand
of tamarack and tall pine

that borders the forest road
and hovers over the bridge

spanning the creek
and there is no breeze

or breath but mine
all silence except for

the tiny change of pressure
as flakes pass my ear

or the slight sizzle as they touch
down on my head and shoulder

or the more distant sound
as subtle as dust accumulating

on the mantle piece
of snow gathering on limb and leaf

and even my steps are muted
by the years that have passed

and muted also is the reason
I am walking here

but the memory ephemeral
as the fragile snow feathery

as the tamarack leaf peculiar
in its persistence

flickers and fades
flickers and fades

then passes as an old photo
passes in an album

I WOULD STEP INTO THE WOODEN BOAT

I would step into the wooden boat
pull up the near shore of the Pend Oreille
along the marshes with the white stumps
of trees that once stood on drier ground
but had succumbed to the water's inundation
now perches for water birds and crows
resting from flight or warily watching my alien work
and if not on the river hike high up the hill
overlooking the big bend where the river turns east
to a side hill clearing logged of its fir
where a large rock clings suggesting a place to sit
and look down the valley
almost to the old Diamond Match mill at Cusick
and brood in the style of a 19th century novel
forgetting the trivialities of model airplanes
or my collection of stamps deliberations
I set aside for the pew and the pastor's sermon

MY FATHER'S WAR

I

The humming birds came to his feeder
regularly enough that he knew each one

by sight he didn't name them but recognized
their coloring and habits of interaction

and he looked for them to return each day
to the yellow plastic flowers and the holes

where they poked their little beaks
for a sip of red sugar nectar

and when they didn't return
and it was clear that they would never return

he would go sit in an old folding chair
under the apricot tree remember

standing near the tower looking east
counting his big silver birds as they returned

noting the numbers on their tall tails
and their peculiar markings

II

I see him mopping up the blood
of an 18-year-old gunner

pooled up against the fuselage ribs
under the wooden floorboards

some of it still frozen in fingered patterns
ice crystals visible on the dark surface

his own blood retreating from his skin
until he is the cabin deep in the woods

doors and windows frozen shut
only a thin curl of smoke in the chimney

and in some interior room sits an old man
hunched over a small stove
warming his cold hands

III

He laid his ear
against the cool skin
of the fuselage

reaching blind
into a handful of wire
cut up

by a 20 mm shell
from a 109
he heard it

like he'd heard it
before
the rumble

of the big
Wright Cyclone engines
the whine

of the 109
piercing the formation
cannons

pounding tracers
leading to the target
a shell parting

the thin aluminum
bursting
in the soft tissue

of the left waist gunner
ripping out
the heart that fueled

his boyish smile
the rattle of bone
flecking

against the metal
near his ear

IV

My father and I climbed the long stairway together
but in his mind we were ascending

a path tangled with vines and giant leaves
all dripping in a sticky stifling mist

heady with the odor of rotting wood
and the calls of strange birds

and as he reached the summit
a familiar smoke appeared putrid

with burnt flesh and punctuated
with the cries of the wounded

I was slightly behind and to his left
climbing the long stairway

into the gallery of Reynolds Store for Men
to sit at Mr. Reynolds' big oak desk

where I would sign for my wallet-sized
official U.S. government ticket

to manhood

LADY SLIPPER

Crossing State Hwy 20 that follows
the spring flow of the Pend Oreille

we hike an old logging road
past the rotting log cabin and up the hill

take in the damp May woods
I had often explored

I wanted to show my mother
a lady slipper

I had stumbled upon
the day before blooming

under a stand of young fir
bearing right where the road splits

and walking maybe another 25 yards
we veer off under the gray-green canopy

shift between the trunks
to stand over a single pink flower

framed by a single ovate leaf
persevering in a molding mat of rusty duff

my mother kneels
I kneel beside her

WOODSHED

In June we began filling the woodshed
        with fir taken from the forest
                that surrounded us,

chunked, carried
        to the pile outside the shed
                where Dad

spent days splitting rounds
        with the big double-edged axe
                he'd bought in Newport.

This was his wordless duty:
        the hefting of the blade,
                the swing over his head,

left hand sliding down
        to join his right
                at the end of the handle,

arms extended, the blade
        gaining speed,
                driving through the wood,

throwing the sundered pieces
        into piles on either side,
                the blade sticking

in the chopping block;
        his mind working
                out the details

of some plan
        to repair the old Ford truck
                or build a roost

for the chickens;
        each fracture
                underscoring some figure,

crossing out another,
        throwing a circle around
                a great idea.

I worked quietly
        alongside him, loaded up
                arms full of pine slabs,

took them into the shed
        and stacked them
                floor to ceiling,
                        ten rows deep.

MY MOTHER BURNED MY FATHER'S LETTERS FROM THE WAR

the smoke rising
from the burn barrel

smoke
mixed with the smoke

of butter wrappers
and banana peels

the censored words
interstitial meanings

calcined

so that no priestly gathering in
of this incense

will bring them back
for this smoke

ascends to the gods
who know every word

but will not tell me

WHERE I WAS WHEN I HEARD ABOUT
THE SINKING OF THE ANDREA DORIA

On July 25, 1956, the Italian liner Andrea Doria,
one of the last luxury ocean liners, collided
with the SS Stockholm off Cape Cod and sank
within twelve hours. 46 died. 1660 were rescued.

My mother told me as we were crossing
the Stratford Rd. bridge coming into town.

I was sitting in the big back seat of the old Chevy
running my fingers over the mohair nap;

the window was down, the bridge smelled
of creosote, the lake looked deep and still;

then my mother put out her arm to signal
and we turned right into Broadway.

DEADEYE

To my mother the teacher.

The cool rotating of her head
the meeting of the eyes

that pause
the silence

a silence where
you can hear your heart

beating inside your head
and you think it makes

the whole room pulsate
and the other children

turning toward you
horror on their faces

grateful it wasn't them

SHORT BLOCK

When Dad brought the car home from the shop,
some men from the neighborhood came by
to stand around the open beak-like hood,
gesticulating, leaning in by turns
to admire the thing. I stood there too
on tiptoe in this colloquium of experts,
lying over the great white fender,
looking down, scanning that yawning space.
Another 50,000 Dad said.
Easy said Mr. Mentti.
Easy I repeated.

'59 CADILLAC

I was standing on the curb across from Sigman's
where my mother had sent me to buy vinegar
when I saw my first '59 Cadillac.

It was coming toward me down 3rd Avenue,
and of all the colors it might have been, it was pink,
the color they say makes violent criminals placid;

maybe that's why it made me weak in the knees
as it slid by, taking at least a minute
to move past; the unbearably prolonged fender,

a lake of glass gently rising to the thin roof
floating deceptively self supported,
sliding back to the sloping rear window

which flowed into an acre of rear deck. Then
without warning, those supercilious fins,
a nightmare only an ichthyologist could dream up.

Of course I wouldn't have used *supercilious*
or *ichthyologist* when I was nine years old,
but these words were on the tip of my tongue.

ROCKING CHAIR REGATTA

We stood among strangers from the town
looking into the storefront window

of Dick's Furniture and Appliance.
It was dark and we were warmly dressed,

adults and taller children behind me
like a group of carolers about to sing,

commenting without taking
our eyes off the two women

rocking in wooden rocking chairs,
groggy, but determined, and according

to KSEM, were six days into the contest
to win the Maytag washer placed

between them and wrapped
with a wide red ribbon and a big red bow.

From down the street, we could hear
the ringing of a Salvation Army bell

in front of Woolworths five and dime.

WE WORE THE KIND OF SHOE

We wore the kind of shoe that could handle
the old metal skates: brown leather high tops,
with a leather sole, something those front clamps
could get hold of, and a heel that fit solidly
into the rear slot, and uppers that could shield
the strap across the ankle. We'd sit
on the front lawn, put on our skates,
jump to the sidewalk and off we'd go
down Gem to B St., around the block
past the Mormon Church behind us on Rose,
rest a moment on a short retaining wall
about half the distance, then roar
the rest of the way, metal wheels on cement
sounding like jet engines in our ears;
take the corner at A, pass Johnny Smith's house,
then race up to Gem and back home, where
we would remove our skates, giggle
at the vibrating numbness in our feet,
and feel two inches shorter.

SINGING DYLAN

I had a cheap guitar
(good enough for Dylan)
and a first-rate imagination;

Dave thought he could sing,
so we hollered
The Times They Are A-Changin'

in my breezeway,
belting child rebellion
and a whole new order,

playing with such sincerity
to the green plaster wall,
when my father walked through,

reminding me I needed to finish
mowing the lawn.

LEICA

I have a photo of my mother my father
took on a sunny spring day,
the day after he returned from a year

in Iceland. She is sitting on a large
granite boulder, the kind that cover the hills
around our Southern California town;

she is about forty two, not a streak
of gray in her dark brown hair;
she is calm and removed, looking

out over the valley. I imagine my father
considering her there, pulling the leather
cover off his new Leica, setting the f-stop,

lifting the camera to his eye,
gathering my mother into the lens,
bringing her resolute profile into focus,

then, after caressing the shutter release
for just the briefest moment, with the weight
of a finger tip, pulling her toward him.

ANOTHER VIEW

My mother is sitting on a large stone
bordered by button sage;

I'm standing near her, leaning,
my arm resting in her lap. We are looking

like Mary and the boy Christ gazing off
into the future, symbolic weeds growing

around my feet, the sun creating
a halo around my blond head, around

her dark brown hair. Her cotton
dress flows down over the stone

in folds as if arranged by attending angels;
the clasps on my little suspenders shine

like gold medallions sewn
into the multi-colored stripes of my t-shirt.

If I look at this photo long enough,
it opens like an ancient altarpiece

to scenes of heaven that include
our house, the old Chevy,
and the apricot orchard.

BEHIND THE DRAWN CURTAIN WITH LIGHT

My father died alone lying
behind the drawn curtain with light
from the aluminum-framed window
reflecting on waxed linoleum

nurses gliding up and down
the hall past his door
bearing water and solace
to the hopeful and the young

My father once told me
that my grandfather
in his last moments
had heard singing

Did my father hear singing
or just the television in the next room

FISHING

The river, released from winter ice-grip
flowed gray like the sky,
like the gray-weathered wood
of the dock where Dad and I stood,
poles limbered, line and lure
ready to be shot over the slate surface,
to sink like a depth charge into a world below
our jurisdiction. And we both dreamed
in the quiet ritual of *thwack* and *whirr*
that a brash German brown would flout
the fish lore and the dark warnings.

MAIN STREET

Mom would turn our 49 Chevy into traffic,
synchronizing clutch and the big lever
on the column, whine first till Sigman's,
make second at Woolworths, third near Rexall Drug.

I would stand behind her on the hump
where the vast front seat-back splits,
sense her turquoise shoulder,
her dark-brown hair tangled by the wind,

vaguely to the left of a foreshortened Main Street,
vivid and lively, cropped by the binocular
of a sloped, divided windshield
and floating on the long white hood

whose chromed missile parted the heat
of the glass-sheeted macadam,
slant-lined for the tidy sorting
of sturdy DeSotos and bat-winged Cadillacs.

'49 CHEVY

He looked like our 49 Chevy,
the austere model without the chrome;
lots of room under the hood
for the diehard theories;
a gaping trunk
with a few laughs and a handy rage;
a big wheel with three on the column
to steer clear of intimacy.

I have this image in my head:
I'm out in front somehow,
impossibly floating,
looking back through the windshield.
He's gripping the wheel, about 50,
thick, graying, auburn hair,
dark, full eyebrows,
eyes on the road;
he's by himself,
doesn't know I'm there.

He sold the old Chevy
for a hundred bucks to a friend
who put it up on blocks
and left it there.

MY FATHER'S GARDEN

My father's garden marched from east to west
on a parade ground of hard-packed granite earth;
the flight aligned, each squash and bean right dressed
with rows bermed deep and straight from south to north.
He ordered halt and each plant crisply snapped
to attention in a loam he prepared with the molded duff
of the sweetgum tree, shoveled, laid, and wrapped
in the hard-packed soil till the soil was rich enough.
And every morning and evening a strict drill:
inspect the ranks with the swagger of a sergeant, correct
the stance of a cavalier tomato, bending its will,
or strip a rotted stem off the zucchini with unchecked
reproach—under command for the good of all,
to fill the commissary stores in the fall.

WE DROVE EAST ON HIGHWAY 10 TO RITZVILLE

then south on 395
to the Tri-Cities,
crossed the Columbia River
just south of Pasco.

I knew the route we'd take;
Dad rehearsed it, map
on the table, weeks before;
made a big plywood box

for the top of our 49 Chevy
to hold the camping gear,
painted it gray.
I recall the 3 a.m. start,

sitting forward a bit
looking over the edge of the window
rolled down in the desert heat,
the sun washing away the gray dawn,

the white guardrail posts
snapping out a mesmeric tattoo,
the odor of warm sagebrush,
a fragment of a meadowlark's song,

the basalt cliffs along the Columbia,
the open pine woods south of Bend
and Klamath Falls and Weed
and Redding—then east on 44

to Lassen Volcanic National Park.
When I would tell people about it later
I said the full name:
Lassen Volcanic National Park.

* * * *

Lassen Volcanic National Park.
We camped on Kings Creek,
the four of us huddled
in an oiled-canvas tent,

the umbrella-type with center pole
Dad comically erected
with a lot of sanitized expletives;
about froze to death

in too-thin sleeping bags
on the too-hard ground,
emerged to a near frost,
ate hot bacon and pancakes

against the morning cold;
waited for the sun
to warm the pines and the
grasses along the creek.

* * * *

Lassen Volcanic National Park.
I think we were in danger there,
a dormant kind of danger
no one would admit:

A trail led from Kings Creek
to Bumpass Hell.
We walked there one sunny morning,
stood high above looking down,

down into calderas
of bubbling sulfurous ooze.
And I learned from a little plaque
that the same compressed heat

that caused this hellish scene
had caused Lassen to explode
sometime in 1915,
sending molten rocks

bouncing down from the peak,
a droll image in a way, still,
I wondered how we could
stand there with such calm.

But Mom and Dad were calm.
My sister was calm.
The ranger was calm.
So I was calm.

* * * *

Lassen Volcanic National Park.
I have a memory of the old lodge
and the big pines as we left the park.
I stood on the hump behind the front seat,

everything gray in the pre-dawn.
Mom had let me pick out a souvenir:
a little pennant with red ties,
attached to a blue felt edge,

a painted picture of the peak
squeezed onto a triangle of blue felt.
It's still in a box
somewhere in the basement.

* * * *

Lassen Volcanic National Park.
Today I found the park's website,
downloaded a map,
moved the cursor

to the dot at Kings Creek,
clicked till it filled the screen.
I had almost expected to see
an eight-year-old

playing near the water.

THE SINGER

Mom hunched over the thing,
hands flying over the levers and wheels,

the needle pumping
through a whole length of cloth,

speed controlled by a lever
she nudged with her knee,

the bobbin taking on thread
from the high wooden spool

down into its hidden chamber
where great pistons pounded

and glistening shirtless men
shoveled coal into throbbing boilers

near giant pulleys and flapping belts.
Later I would sit on the stool,

turn the flywheel, move the presser foot
up and down, push the power lever

just a hair to hear the motor grind;
Mom would scold—who knows

how many men I injured.

LIFE SCROLL

She marked her life on a scroll
shouldered in a sheath of memory.

At times she'd lift it out,
roll back to younger days,

show us some portrait of past
remorse, a stinging word,

a study in native reserve,
a failure to succeed.

At night we'd see her add
another foot or two,

but not before she'd turn
to an earlier sketch, select

the self-muting colors,
the agonizing shapes,

the hopeful lines that draw
meaning from ruthless events

to echo in familiar forms—
the past sounding in the present

like ancient carillon bells
rung at daily Vespers,

their cracks and casting flaws
resounding.

LEGACY

Which of us deserves a perfect father?
The man who is himself the perfect son.
And who presumes his father be the better
part of Gandhi, Lee, and Washington?
The son who's overcome with flawless art
the ways and bents and firm proclivities
inscribed on family chromosomes that chart
our good along with darker tendencies.
To blame the man for failings he possessed
will not forgive the umbrage that you bear;
the anger in the end will only wrest
from gene and life a rocky thoroughfare.
And be aware your father's worst abuse
may rise in you and be your son's excuse.

IF I COULD I WOULD MEET MY FATHER

If I could, I would meet my father
for a beer at The Anchor,
ask him a lot of questions
about his life with my mother,
the war, why he didn't like children;
and I wouldn't blame him for anything,
and after the second or third beer,
laugh and be silly, the alcohol
reducing the accumulated weight
of our failures; and we would weave
our way home, see my mother
disgusted, grown Christian men, happy,
my father's arm draped over my shoulder
as we slur a drunk's cantillation.

Part Two: Life in Vegas

How could I be envious of youth?
I tell you from the start the young face trouble.

MEMORIES STACK UP

like cordwood
drying between
the trunks of two oaks
and sometimes
you can remove
a single piece
in a way
that does not unsettle the others
hold it in your hands
feel its weight
its rough bark
and splintered edges
marks from the saw
where it was severed
from its place
in a live tree
reassembled here
out of order
and when you have had enough
you put it back in its place
and maybe a splinter
has pricked a finger
or some sawdust
remains
on your clothes

WE LEAVE OUR MARK

Think of a funeral not as an emblem
of misfortune but a commemoration
not that life was cut short
as in the death of a child
but that the child had lived at all
and for the nonagenarian
that she had lived long
and in any case we leave our mark
(and this should be noted and celebrated)
if only the stretched belly of our mother
or a lost toy buried near the porch
maybe a depression in the ground
where we once dug a hole
and didn't quite fill it in
maybe a tree we planted that will last
a hundred years
an addition to the house
a word in anger
an approving smile
the bearing of children

FUNERALS

Funerals exhilarate me,
not in the sense of being happy,
but more vigorous and alive;
motivated to make the bed,
change the oil in my car,
plant an azalea,
learn a new bluegrass lick,
read the biography of Harry Truman,
serve well in my community;
and document it all in snapshots
for my survivors
to pin on a poster
at my funeral.

TO NOTE THE SACRED PLACES WE BEGAN

Here is this small marker on the wall
at the head of the marriage bed, and this little plaque
over a porcelain tub or above the horse's stall;
and on the small back seat of a Capri in black
this embroidered date near an empty bottle of Chablis,
and these rough-carved letters in a heart-shaped shield
at the lower crotch of a backyard maple tree
and this remembrance stone in a daisy field.
If the minion's grave is marked, and cenotaphs
are raised to tribute mayors, monks, and monarchs;
and a dirge is sung at death, or epitaphs
and elegies appear on local landmarks,
it might be good, in honoring life's hard span,
to note the sacred places we began.

'32 FREIGHTLINER

Sometimes I wonder
if the car that will collide with mine
in a spectacular head-on is

at the stoplight next to me
on a trajectory to hit me
this afternoon or next week

or next year maybe when I'm 83
that idling blue '09 Dodge
recycled remade will skid

toward me as a red '31 Ford
or a black '32 Freightliner

I AM WATCHING SIX-YEAR-OLDS PLAY SOCCER

I am watching 6-year-olds play soccer
while cumulonimbus clouds rise up
in formation out of the northwest,
out over the blue-green oaks
to become a stream of corpulent B-17s
on their way to bomb Minneapolis.
I know the sirens are screaming.
People must be processing to shelters,
for the machines of terror move relentlessly
southeast, across the western sky.
And now I can hear the big flack guns
in the south sending up blooms
of black laden with flesh-shredding iron.
But nothing is more urgent than this orb, besides,
tonight we'll see the wreckage on the evening news.

A MOMENT YEARS AGO TODAY

We are lying next to each other
gauging the limits of youthful passion
when I am momentarily distracted

wondering if we would be
like the little figures of a bride and groom
from your parents wedding cake

that now stand yellowed on a shelf
in their hall closet so calm
and steady though a bit pale

he in a black suit she in a long gown
he looks responsible and employed
she has her arm hooked at his left elbow

standing slightly behind yet not meekly
ready for the domestic life that awaits her
both looking middle aged somehow

or maybe just constant and solid
joined as they are at the shoulder and hip—
I lay my head on your breast.

REFLECTIONS ON MY WEDDING DAY

I

I bathed
in her grandmother's
bare basement

a showerhead over a drain
no curtain
my nude body

exposed
by the dim blue light
from a soiled pane

framed up
against the ceiling joists
and a single 40w bulb

hanging
from a length of wire
over a rusty utility sink

pail peach-colored flesh
against the dull gray
cinder block walls

and the darkened fir steps
I had descended

II

We ordered a single Ruben sandwich,
killed off some time watching

Olympic wrestling
I met room service at the door

took the sandwich
didn't offer a tip

stood for a while
looking out over the city

noted my bride slipping off
to the bathroom

knowing
she would soon reappear

a sachet of myrrh
resting between her breasts

her hair like a flock of goats
descending from Gilead

smelling of henna and aloes
her lips honeyed

and her breath like apples
then I was standing

alone on a very large stage
looking out over

familiar faces
Mom and Dad were there

roommates from school
a college professor

all looking up with expectation
waiting

III

If life is a river this is the place
right after the section
lined with lush meadows
filled with the singing of exotic birds

where the river enters a deep gorge
and night is coming on
and somewhere around midnight
you hear the roar of falls

and even if you could reach the shore
the cliffs come right down
to the water's edge
and as the falls
comes closer
and closer
you say
your final prayers
your heart
beating wildly
and you wait
at dawn you realize you are still alive
having passed a noisy rapids
you barely remember the tumult
happy to be on the other side

THE SCHOLAR TAKES HIS TURN

The scholar takes his turn
at the podium and as he speaks

he occasionally looks toward the faces
of his colleagues sitting in a group

to the left for the solemn nod the frown
the possible look of indifference

and in the back of his mind
as he reads sentences from his paper

he reads this tableau maybe determining
who he will talk with at the coffee break

or who he will sit next to at lunch
and all of this has taken some of the joy

out of his research the reason he got
into this field in the first place or maybe

his wife is sitting in the audience
and she is attentive and she is looking forward

to a pleasant discussion of his work
over dinner and a glass of wine

TABLE GRACE

For the bread you made with your own hands,
sliced, toasted, and buttered;
and the eggs from the chickens you keep in our back yard,
boiled, peeled, set out on the plate;

and the strawberries you picked with our daughter
you made into jam that I spread on my toast;
and for your perpetual presence here with me
gracing our table—

for all of these things I am truly grateful;
but you should know that these words
are the understudies, stand-ins, retained

in lieu of the powerful actors who live in the heights,
whose talents are far above all others;
the ones who move audiences to tears.

REMAINS

When she goes to see her sister
near Seattle and I'm alone

for a few days I think
about what it might be like

if her plane went down
buried in some midwestern pasture

no remains to weep over
just a pair of pajamas on her pillow

maybe a bra hanging from a doorknob
her clothes in the hamper

mingled with mine or a bowl
on the counter with bits

of boiled egg in the bottom
a spoon sitting next to it

perhaps some flecks
of toothpaste on the mirror

a fingerprint on her morning tea cup
strands of her hair in the bathtub drain

DANCING IN MINNEHAHA PARK ON THIS
LATE SULTRY SUMMER AFTERNOON

The band has drifted into dance tunes
on this late sultry summer afternoon
so dance with me you said
dance with that old couple
up by the canopied stage gliding
as one in the waltz
and these two women here laughing
and dipping and swinging
over the crowded floor
in a high-stepping polka
and that middle-aged woman
over there standing to the side
with her frail mother arm in arm
swaying to the two-step
and with this bare-chested old man
in a green kilt and a red plastic lei
fluttering at ease between us all
with a nameless footwork
and a naked humanity.

AND YOU ARE THIS TO ME, A DAPPLED SHADE

Beneath this locust tree a dappled light
that trims the phlox and Susan bud and rims
the lilies with a golden braid despite
the fill of leaves that lace the spreading limbs;
and an equal shade to cool the hosta leaves
and shield the astilbe and the columbine
where in early spring the bleeding heart achieves
prolific bloom when shadow and light combine.
And you are this to me, a dappled shade
and light, above a fertile patch of soil
where flora's seed and root are amply splayed;
your limbs are shelter for the gardener's toil.
I didn't guess the nature of this tree,
but learned its just effect by slow degree.

GARDEN'S END

Today I mark the end of Summer's garden.
The first hard frost has blacked the later fruit
Of all but the beets and Brussels sprouts that harden
To the cold until the cold is absolute.
And though the foliage long ago expired,
Potatoes wait my fork to probe and raise
Them from the still-warm earth, but since I'm tired
From harvest's work, they'll wait a few more days.
Before the snow I'll pull the flagging corn,
The slimy Early Girls, the browning beans
And burn their spent remains till they're reborn
In useful ash, then rest from strict routines
To gratefully consume the cellared yield
And plan another crop to fill the field.

GO, LOVELY WEED

I've started leaving some of the weeds in the garden,
the ones that have a pleasing flower or shape
like ladies thumb and goldenrod and mullein.
The cow vetch and the campion escape
my hoe most of the time and I will mow
around the hoary alyssum in the lawn
or even let some dandelions flow
along the garden edge till the flower's gone.
In some locales the morning glory's a pest
and honeysuckle sometime gets the ax
which makes me wonder who devised the test
for weed that prompts obsessive plant attacks.
Go, lovely weed—tell them that waste their time
in mere eradication, you're sublime.

DREAMS OF WOLVES

She stands in the prisoner's dock, small and pale,
eclipsed by shadows that these tabernacles
cast. The black-robed judge, the hard-oak rail,
the burly bailiff, china wrists in shackles,
play like a courtroom scene from Law and Order;
but we're sitting here and she's up there
beside her somber court-appointed lawyer.
Save the spectacle, the drama's hard to bear.

The apple tree you used to climb's in bloom.
Your Shakespeare and your Tolkien rest with grace
on bookends, gathered from your silent room.
Radiant stars above your bed still chase
the dark as you hoped they would in dreaded midnight
when wolves in dreams would come to steal your birthright.

AN INSOLENT DEMAND

You face the dawn and shake your little fist;
and when the sun appears, as is its course,
you look the conquering, grinning Bolshevist
and think you've made it rise by threat of force.
Likewise the moon gives grudgingly its light
and tidal benefit; and runs its path,
or so you think, in deference to your sulfite
provocation and propitious wrath.
What grave remorse has altered love's intent?
What anguish turned an earnest gift to dung?
Could memory of a vague abandonment
have roused your painfully acerbic tongue?
Or why does love held in an open hand
provoke in you an insolent demand?

GREEN OLIVES

She would move
through the salad bar,
take two green olives,

always two green olives
the ones with pimento
stuffed in the hole

where the pit used to be—
Now I do the same,
always two green olives.

They are a rage of bitterness
in the mouth, bold, impudent,
a vitriol that arrests me;

for a moment I cannot speak,
stunned by their blunt wrath
and brute passion—tomorrow

I will take two green olives;
eat the first in remembrance,
the second in grief.

YOU SLIP INTO THIS WORLD HEADFIRST

for Liam Gregory Smith

You slip into this world headfirst
like the soft-ripe banana slips

from its blackened case when squeezed
and likewise at your peak ripe awash

in the bloodied river of your escape
a fragment of the amniotic sack still

covering your head and face like a thief
wears pantyhose but quickly unmasked

all blue still tethered like an astronaut
to the mother-ship free but in alternate

space once in suspension now seized
by hands that clutch and draw you down

against your mother's breast and light
more than your eyes can take in and breath

to fill the sucking void of your lungs and sounds
once muffled as one hears in a pool

now vivid with yet unknown words
of wonder welcome and joy

MOVING HOME

It starts with some kind of breakdown
work money love and the next

thing you know they are there
in your basement maybe they don't

ask they just appear one day
with their clothes their kids a grocery

bag of TV dinners and now
a half-eaten taco in the wrapper

edges out from under the couch
maybe a soiled diaper betrays

its hiding place under a bed
and small toys threaten

bodily harm in the night
and your furnace fan pumps

their fear or despair or rancor
through the ducts to every corner

of the house but it's temporary
they say and you say it's temporary

and you wait maybe in anguish
you open a window or two

to air the place out.

LIFE IN VEGAS

How could I be envious of youth?
I tell you from the start the young face trouble;
and if they'd stop to hear the abject truth,
would head for Vegas, do it on the double,
and stay there till their hair is gray as steel.
Why Vegas? Gambling there's a simple matter
of pulling a lever or spinning a roulette wheel,
no spouse, no kids, no job, no dog to batter
and fleece your soul. Yes, I would recommend
Las Vegas. The slot machines never need paint,
the women are eternally firm and waiters attend
to all the chores and life has no restraint.
I wish I had known this when I was twenty two.
I sometimes long for life that's thin and untrue.

EVENING ON RUBY BEACH

A photographer is coaxing the last bit of light
into a lens—the reflection of trees
crowded onto a back-water pool

fed by a mountain stream making its way
over sand to meet the surf
sighing along the stony beach.

There are fishermen standing in the waves
with long poles and big reels
casting lead and bait out beyond the swells,

and the smelt takers are arriving with nets
to get an early start on the night's catch.
Large rock shapes silhouetted

against the slowly darkening western sky
speak of another time, or maybe no time,
so we sit on a log by a fire

of driftwood, the flames
creating a little dome of orange light
in a blue-gray dusk.

Part Three: How to Learn

*Warm your hands
over this small flame*

STARBUCKS, TUESDAY, 3:36 P.M.

An ex-con brags to his cronies,
loudly backing religion
and telling dirty jokes

while a middle-aged guy in sunglasses
leers at teenage girls
giggling in their caramel macchiatos.

The entrance of a single mother,
breasts pouting, daughter
clinging to her skirt,

arrests a sottish vagrant's
mumbling, but doesn't stop
his ejaculating a loud *hey*

which unnerves the old lady
stirring cream into her medium
dark-roast-of-the-day.

And across from me a young women
in a black trench coat sees nothing;
writes urgently in a little book

filling pages in fine print—
seems she's unaware
that her latte's getting cold.

READING FOR PLEASURE AT BARNES AND NOBLE

A man about my age
gray scruffy beard
well-worn red plaid flannel shirt
wide open to a white v-neck
with coffee stains at the belly
sits across from me
holding Michener's *Texas*
with the bulk of the heavy volume
resting in his right hand
while his left delicately holds open
six or so pages and
after a few minutes he pauses
to consider the weight of it
runs his thumb
across the unread remainder
looks at the last page for a moment
then closes the book
lays it on the nearby table
as if to say his coffee
won't last that long

ME AS JIMMY STEWART

I'm smoking a pipe

the bowl reclining in my left hand
my worsted wool coat open

an ample silk tie pointing
to the top of true-waisted gabardines

pleated and full right hand tucked
into a pocket holding back the coat tail

a shoulder against a lamppost the smoke
curling up under the brim of a fedora

that covers a slick pompadour then I waste
some time reading headlines

at the news stand on the corner
of Broadway and 3rd eventually board

the subway for Central Park
mount a carved-wooden horse

on the old merry-go-round
smoke trailing over the herd

THE PHONE SOLICITOR

I imagine her by the pool
sipping a mojito as she greets me

in a rum-softened voice
and asks me how life is treating me

and commenting on how beautiful
the day is where she is and hoping it

is as beautiful where I am and saying
the reason I'm calling Mr. Rhoads

with a minty tone and as she reads
her script the sound of her voice is no

longer strained through the tiny
speaker of my phone but full bodied

and a door opens up to palm
trees and exotic birds perched here

and there in a perfumed breeze
and I am now lounging next to her

in a pool-side chair where her tan
distracts me just enough that

when she leans over to offer
me the pen I sign

ACTION STILL

After a football action photo
in the St. Paul Pioneer Press

T. Williamson floats on the stadium air,
his arms high extended, his fingers aflare.
The NFL football hangs plump as a peach
just ripe for the plucking and well within reach.

Poteat, the defender, is fully laid out
a foot off the turf, he's thinking (no doubt):
"I've got a good grip on T. Williamson's knee
but, damn, that's the goal line ablur under me."

And in the same photo, a sideline tableau:
Two fans mouthing *Yes* and one mouthing *No*;
three cheerleaders, breasts in a heaving upswing;
the ref in position to judge the whole thing.

HISTORY IN A PIECE OF CHALK

Pick up a piece of chalk
from the narrow blackboard shelf,

examine the facets of its tip,
or the fractured end

where it snapped off in the hand
of an eager scribe; put it

up to your ear, listen
for the symbols scratched

on the dusty gray surface:
the advanced formula subtracting

its substance, the stout words
of the Gettysburg Address grinding

it down to this sharp point, maybe,
I will not talk in class. I will

not talk in class. I will not talk
in class droning in a drooping

cloud of dust, prompting
a dry cough, clinging

to sweaty little fingers.

TELECOM'S BEQUEST

A new technology does not add or subtract something.
It changes everything. Neil Postman

To announce the dawn of his tele-technology,
Morse sent a line from the Holy Muse:
"What *hath* God wrought!" he tapped (in apology),
and opened an epoch of noxious news.

BEFORE GESTALT

Do you remember when every chair
was different when each chair
was a new object to be explored
with your hands or your mouth or your feet
back before you could say chair or cared to say chair
before chair was simply a functional descriptor
before you said look at those chairs
before you knew seat or rung
or back or slat or leg
when the room contained mounds
of softness or lumps of roughness
or hard and smooth with flat at eye level
and tall rectangular of bright and dark
where the dark was solid
and the bright offered no resistance
and dark hurt when you hit
your head on it, and the tall bright
when you put your had into it
would sometime grip and not let go
and the room might be full of smooth and rough
and hard and tall and flat and dark and bright

THEATRE FOR STRANGERS

You would break out of this tiny and tawdry theatre
in which your own plot is always being played,
and you would find yourself under a freer sky,
in a street full of splendid strangers. G. K. Chesterton

As the curtain rises a man begins to fondle
a battered chainsaw leaking oil on the asphalt
next to an old couch; not far from him
a young mother examines a high chair with bits
of dried cereal taking cover in the hidden places,
while an old woman scanning a table of figurines
embraces a brand new vinyl shower curtain
still boxed with original price tag;
                                        they don't know
each other; they don't know they are actors;
they don't know they are on a stage; they don't see
me sitting under the maple tree sipping
a beer; they don't see I'm reading Chesterton.
Maybe it's the beer; maybe it's Chesterton.

PLANTAIN

Make peace with the persistent plantain—
interloper in the hallowed lawn.
Set it free in the garden plot
and it will lift leaves in ample thanksgiving.

Ancient apothecaries knew its powers—
cures forgotten by urbane suburbanites
who openly plot its overthrow
with a malediction and a murderous eye.

Even Dürer knew its measure—
a healing balm, a sign of blood;
and chose to lay its prophetic portrait
at the feet of the Holy Mother and Child.

So let it live as cure and symbol;
consider its once reverenced place.
Take its relentless tenacity for hope
and its history as surety of life.

SOULS THAT HAVE LANGUISHED IN ATTICS

Three-fifty each for these orphaned
portraits, sepia-toned, on cards
where smiles were prohibited,

standing upright in a rusting tackle box
on this chrome-and-yellow-vinyl
table next to a potato masher

and a table lamp, black ceramic
in the likeness of a prowling panther,
no shade. It seems sad, them ending up here,

as if the notion that souls can be captured
in a likeness were true; and here are the souls
of this child perched in a wicker chair

and this somber farm family, arranged
in front of a painted Athenian scene;
a bride and groom, him seated, her hand

on his shoulder, looking ill at ease; and now
as I tilt each portrait toward me, the souls
of these long dead eddy around me,

souls that have languished in attics, just waiting
for someone to welcome them home,
or maybe just to stand here a moment

and grieve over their abandonment.

HOW TO LEARN

Warm your hands
over this small flame

feel the heat
prickle your face

pick up a few coals
and put them

in your breast pocket
let them burn through

to make a scar
over your heart

stay leave
your collecting

of cold stones
with which you are apt

to fill your pockets
then discard when

the journey's over

RODNEY PRESBYTERIAN CHURCH C. 1850

The Presbyterian Church in Rodney, Mississippi sits
on a hill above the flood plain and is one of the few buildings
that survived recent inundations of the Mississippi River. Partially
restored in the 1990s, it is now abandoned, ripe for exploration.

We descend into Rodney
slipping under the flood
of time as it washes away
past deeds but has left
this parable in wood and brick
a narrow stair steep and curving
entered not from the ample front
entrance with its double doors
and its wide formal steps
but from a side door
discrete hidden separate
leading to the gallery pushed up
against the ceiling
I ascend to hear the soft moaning
and the brush of calloused feet
and feel the swaying swathed
in the musk of sorrow
and look down on the large box pews
where families fathers and mothers
children shrouded
in gardenia and magnolia sit
under the light of the high windows
under the raised white pulpit
where the preacher reads
the words of Jesus
Come unto me all ye that labour
and are heavy laden
and I will give you rest

LAND OF REST

The old stone wall runs to the west
past the flowering crab and the cedar tree,
up to the farm-house hill where it comes to rest
quite suddenly in a makeshift rockery.

I walked its length to ponder the mason's craft,
stone on stone in made-up courses, improvised
it seems, or laid up as if to draft
a map to a place not yet materialized

but seen in the stooped farmer's mystical eye:
a place free of the endless bending toil
to clear the rocky ground for the corn and rye
that sustains a life dependent on the soil;

a land that waves of lined-out hymns proclaim
to weary souls, who view its endless store
and gentle rest, and see no walls to frame
its fertile fields, nor stones to build them for.

EVEN THE ANIMALS

O great mystery and wonderful sacrament,
that animals should see the new-born Lord
lying in a manger. From a responsorial chant
for Matins of Christmas

But ask the animals, and they will teach you. . . .
Which of all these does not know that the hand
of the LORD has done this? Job 12:7,9

The sheep lay still under cool eastern skies
and looked up at the promising stars with a stare
that so absorbed the sharp-eyed shepherds they likewise
turned eyes upward in the darkened air,

then looked back at the sheep now oddly haloed
with wooly beams and looked so serene
the wary shepherds probed the portent, elbowed
each other with talk of what this thing might mean.

When angels came these modest men forgot
their query; were racked so much with terror
a cherub had to calm them with the thought
that they should look to the sheep to see their error,

whose manner had not changed except they'd stood
and turned in longing toward the singing seraph
to gaze at the brilliant light as best they could
as if the light itself was feed enough.

At the angels charge the shepherds ran to pose
this first of countless scenes, *tableau vivant,*
to honor the ruddy child in swaddling clothes,
unlikely deity, *le Dieu Enfant.*

The scene struck, the shepherds, returning to the fold
in half-crazed joy, took a moment to once more weigh,
amid stories of babe and manger that were told,
the import of their flock's weird display.

Then one recalled that the stabled cows had gathered round
to stand between the shepherds kneeling on the floor,
had held their cud and stopped their lowing sound.
What mystery that even the animals see and adore.

PRAYER FOR THOSE WHO FALL FROM THE SKY

And the Lord said, "I will cause all my goodness
to pass in front of you . . . but," he said, "you cannot
see my face, for no one may see me and live."
Exodus 33:19, 20

From that first moment, the dip of the nose, the yaw
to the left, a thump, some smoke, the engines' exhaled
breath, the pilot's flat voice: all systems have failed,
and utter panic rakes the cabin like a claw:

may grace descend with you and with these strangers,
and as, we assume, your life replays, mundane,
hilarious, appalling, may the certainty of death constrain
your desperate heart, for the dead can face no dangers;

and may you in that last howling second trace
what Moses on Sinai could not see, and live;
what most in meager worldly bliss misgive:
the fearsome goodness of God's face.

THE SUN HAS RISEN ON MY COARSE COMPLAINT

. . . the sun of righteousness will rise
with healing in its wings. Malachi 4:2

The Sun has risen on my coarse complaint:
that discontent drives its root
in a fertile slough of seamy unrestraint
till it bears ample fruit

that swells and bursts to scatter fecund seed
which sprouts and blooms and bears a crop
prolific as the first before my greed
can taste a single drop.

To think exposure breaks the Adamic curse
presumes the power to repent.
This light disrobes my rank intent and worse:
a famine of lament.

But what the Sun convicts of flagrant crime,
the restless raging bent toward lust,
it calcines till the proof is dust and I'm
left—mercifully—just.

PRAYER FOR THE RICH AND THE POOR

Philippians 4:11–13

I ask for contentment first for you both
are prone to covet one has

and is never satisfied the other has not
and looks in longing toward those who have

and for an eye for someone near who is in need
that from your resources abundant

or meager you will give a lot or a little
as was given to you either by hard

work or by inheritance and then for joy
that in your daily walk in this world

you would not be troubled by want or wealth
but treasure the grace of God

LUX AETERNA

Gettysburg, walking the field of Picket's Charge, July 2010

Two hours of artillery have silenced the birds,
and as the smoke worries over the field,
out of the woods lines of men appear
and appear, and appear, till the ground undulates
in bayonet-topped waves that break and close, relentless
in morbid procession toward a treacherous shore
that erupts in sulfurous blasts that tear and erode
so that the lines contract and dissolve into piles
of writhing flesh, a sudden feast of blood
and fresh fluids for the tick and the chigger
that wait in the thick grass.

The dead lie scattered over this wretched field,
all bloated in the summer heat as it is taking days
to dig the graves. The smell is hard to bear.
By now the ticks have returned to blades of grass
to absorb their meal of blood, blood that has thickened
in the vein so that it can no longer be drawn in,
and have given over the corpse to the flies that cover
the eyes, and to their offspring of hungry maggots.

I am stepping over ghost-bodies; not out of need since
they no longer have substance, but out of respect, because
they have lain here these one hundred fifty years for me
to consider how they died and where they died; to mark
each place on the map of my memory so that their suffering
will not be erased by time or carried off
by the hungry wolves of indifference.

Later the fireflies, as if unaware of the intervening years,
cover the darkening field, offspring of a thousand generations,
each one carrying its little lantern, not to light a path,
but as an eternal flame on a grave, one
for every soul that crossed to the other side.

THIS LACONIC MOON

"Good grief," I said. "My problems aren't more
important than the moon." Mary Jane Butters

Who knows
the magic of the moon
with its tug on the tides;
and whatever the myth or magic—
romance, an omen
of good harvest,
the harbinger of doom—
it steps out night after night
onto the firmamental stage,
audiences filing in, filing out:
the fall of Rome,
the atom bomb,
my mother's death.

While I suffer, it shines;
while I sing, it shines;
while it shines there is beginning;
while it shines there is ending;
passing on the light
of another, plotting
the seasons, eclipsing
and being eclipsed.

VITAL MEANING

Romans 1:20

That God could write
with a universe,
prolific, terse,
in matter and light,

is mystery to a creature
who is merely equipped
to read from script,
not by nature,

but by ordinance
in dim-lit rooms
where one assumes
by force of persistence

that ways of knowing
are consigned to books
or study nooks
or forms as limiting.

But the cosmos shouts
a thesis; clear
to all who hear,
there are not doubts

of the hidden character,
the godly quality,
and timeless authority
of the world's Maker.

Not with platitude,
but with a force
that contests the course
of turpitude,

Creation, profuse
with vital meaning,
leaves us reeling—
without excuse.

THE OCCASIONAL FIRE

Rapt, we sit by the occasional fire
watching flames applaud the edges
of a log, reaching up like hands
of a congregation in praise of God.

We converse in calm voices, but frequently
pause to stare in silence; ruddy
faces, crossed with muted reverence;
not knowing why, but communing

with the radiant transubstantiation
of wood to ash, the pulse and glow
of the last fervent dance of wood-atoms
that adjourns the cruel ticking of the clock

till time itself in a dreamy trance,
like smoke drifting among the stars,
curls round and round our tranquil forms
and comes to rest by the occasional fire.

www.ingramcontent.com/pod-product-compliance
Lightning Source LLC
Chambersburg PA
CBHW060421090426

42734CB00011B/2392